A book about wild flowers should be as beautiful as the flowers themselves, and Katherine Mackenzie's lovely watercolors, executed with so much care and love, make **Wild Flowers of the South** a unique field guide as well as a charming art book.

In the eight years she has been painting wild flowers, she has traveled throughout eastern North America, as far north as Devon Island beyond the Arctic Circle, but nothing prepared her for the lavish richness of the South. Perhaps that is why her southern paintings are among the most beautiful she has ever done.

All of the paintings were made from living flowers and they capture the distinctive features of each as well as the individual vitality and charm. Experienced botanists find as much delight in them as do newcomers to the world of wild flowers.

A special treat for both adults and children is the text, which gives some of the stories, odd uses, cures and folklore associated with these flowers.

Wild Flowers
of the
South

Tundra Books

Katherine Mackenzie

Copyright © 1977, Katherine Mackenzie

All rights reserved. No part of this work may be reproduced or transmitted in any form or by any means, electronic or mechanical, including photocopying and recording, or by any information storage or retrieval system, without permission in writing from the publisher.

First printing.

Published by Tundra Books of Northern New York, Plattsburgh, New York 12901

ISBN 0-912766-56-5
12 pre-pack ISBN 0-912766-71-9
Library of Congress Card No. 76-58656

Printed in the United States by Froelich/Greene Inc.

Introduction

In this fully illustrated, pocket-sized volume are descriptions of many wild plants of our region, some common and some rare. The selected species are simply presented in bright water colors for easy recognition and are accompanied by concisely written descriptions providing information likely to be wanted whenever a new flower has been discovered. The author shows a real familiarity with the plants as they grow in their native habitats and with the literature and legend that have developed around each.

For the child or amateur adult, the uncluttered illustrations and straight-forward, simple-to-understand text make the matter of identifying an unknown plant easy. They also tempt the reader to browse through the pages, recall plants recently seen, and search for other plants, hitherto unnoticed.

More than ever before, wild plants and, because of their beauty, wild flowers are the object of widespread interest and appreciation. Whatever contributes to our greater knowledge about them — their names, what they look like, where they grow, when they bloom, etc. — helps us understand their place in the overall scheme of things. We need to act now to preserve them, by implementing a worldwide program of habitat preservation. Toward these ends this little volume makes its contribution.

Wade T. Batson
Distinguished Professor of Biology
University of South Carolina
Columbia, South Carolina

References

Batson, Wade T. (1964) **Wild Flowers in South Carolina**, University of South Carolina Press.

Batson, Wade T. (1975) **Genera of the Eastern Plants** (second edition), The State Printing Company.

Duncan, Wilbur H. and Leonard E. Foote (1975) **Wildflowers of the Southeastern United States**, University of Georgia Press.

Justice, William S. and C. Ritchie Bell (1968) **Wild Flowers of North Carolina**, University of North Carolina Press.

Peterson, Roger Tory and Margaret McKenny (1968) **A Field Guide to Wildflowers of Northeastern and North-central North America**, Houghton Mifflin Company.

A Note from the Author

It was a wonderful experience leaving the ice and snow of a northern winter and driving south. The temperature climbed higher by the hour, the snow gradually disappeared, and from Washington, D.C. on, the drive was sheer delight. It must be hard for Southerners to imagine what it is like to leave behind four months of freezing temperatures, heavy clothes and boots, and three days later see jessamine in bloom all along the highway. I was so eager to look at it, I had trouble staying on the road and out of the ditches. The swamps outside Savannah were particularly exciting with water birds swooping and diving among the reeds and water lilies and singing in the warm sunshine. From the coastal beaches through the plains, Piedmont, into the hills, everywhere I looked, more and more flowers and shrubs seemed to be coming into bloom before my eyes.

I have now painted wild flowers all over the eastern half of North America, from as far north as Devon Island in the High Arctic. The contrast between the tiny, exquisite flowers that bloom briefly in the short Arctic summer and the sumptuous profusion of the long-blooming wild flowers in the South is something I still marvel at.

The beauty of the South in springtime is equaled only by the real and warm kindness of Southerners; I had heard of it as legend, but I now know it to be true. I would especially like to mention Dr. Wade Batson of the University of South Carolina who gave me advice and help, and generously shared with me his special sites of wild flowers — knowledge that has taken him years to accumulate and without which I would have been lost.

This little collection of drawings reflects the pleasure I experienced in that countryside, whose beauty I hope no Southerner takes for granted. Perhaps this book will give encouragement to anyone, young or old, who has never known the excitement of looking for wild flowers, recognizing them, photographing them, drawing them or painting them, to go out and make an album of of his or her own.

Katherine Mackenzie

1 Pink and Violet Wood Sorrel
Oxalis violacea

This early sorrel carpets the woods of North Carolina in spring. The leaves are good to chew or put in salads, but should not be eaten to excess. An extract can be made from the plant that will remove ink stains from linens. This is a pinkish purple sorrel. The flowers grow on stems directly out of small bulbs.

2 Spring Star Flower
Ipheion uniflorum

This bluish star-like spring flower grows above flattened leaves and has a faint onion smell. It escaped from gardens to run wild and decorate not only fields, but even waste places in cities.

3 Sorrel
Rumex hastatulus

Often when driving along country roads in the South, you pass a whole field covered with blooming sorrel. The brown-red hue makes you feel you have come upon something very exotic, and it's a surprise to find that this handsome plant is classified as a weed. The leaves are used in soups and salads. But while it's possible to eat this sorrel, you shouldn't eat much of it as the oxalate in it can become poisonous. Sheep Sorrel, a related species, is grown commercially.

4 Prickly Pear
Opuntia compressa

This cactus can be found in May and June in dry sandy places all the way from Massachusetts to Georgia. The purplish fruit is edible but has to be peeled carefully because it is covered with little prickles. The insect cochineal feeds on this plant.

5 Crested Dwarf Iris
Iris cristata

When in bloom, the flower of this little iris stands above the leaves and is easily seen. Later, the leaves keep on growing to about a foot in length. It blossoms in April and May, and can be found in rich woods all over the southern states. It is very lovely and reminds many people of orchids.

6 Flowering Dogwood
Cornus florida

Dogwood blooming in spring before the leaves come out makes a walk in the woods or a drive down a country road a most pleasurable experience. The bark of the tree can be soaked in whiskey to make a cure for chills and fever. If you want very white teeth, peel a young branch and chew it until it is frayed: then use it as a toothbrush. The wood is very hard and was used for cogs in machinery, wood engravings, and other commercial enterprises before the development of steel and plastics. A red dye can be made from the roots and a black one from the bark. It is the state flower of both North Carolina and Virginia.

7 Toadflax
Linaria canadensis

This delicate blue-to-purple spring flower is actually a common weed that grows all over eastern North America, decorating fields and roadsides. It seems to have a tendency to grow in the most barren places — fallow fields and rocky wastes — coloring them to please the eye. An ointment made from the flower has been used to treat skin irritations.

8 Marsh Pennywort
Hydrocotyle umbellata

Marsh Pennywort is easy to recognize because of the unusual shape of its leaves. The plant grows on the edges of beaches and in ditches, and the leaves are succulent. Only on close examination will you notice the little clusters of tiny whitish flowers.

9 Wild Hyacinth
Camassia scilloides

The Indians called this hyacinth "quamash" and this has been kept in its Latin name. It grows in April and May along streams and scattered through meadows. Its root is a bulb that looks like a small onion and was eaten by the Indians.

10 Rue Anemone
Anemonella thalictroides

This early spring anemone grows in the eastern United States. You can distinguish it from other anemones by the rounded tips of the leaves. Look for it in rich woods from northern Florida all the way to eastern Oklahoma and north.

11 Spring-Beauty
Claytonia virginica

Spring-Beauty is most appropriately named for it is one of the earliest and most delicate of all the spring flowers which grow in rich woods all over eastern North America. Its Latin name is a tribute to John Clayton, a botanist who came to Virginia in 1705. The early tender leaves can be used in salads — they're rich in vitamins, and the starchy root tastes like chestnuts.

12 Dwarf Cinquefoil
Potentilla canadensis

This early spring flower is common from Georgia to Arkansas, Missouri to Kentucky, as well as in the Northeast. You will find it in fields, along the edges of roads and in waste places. It is reputed to have powerful medicinal qualities, and has been made into a tea for stomach aches. It got its Latin name "potentilla" because of its supposed potency against evil spirits that cause fevers.

13 False Garlic
Nothoscordum bivalve

The bulb of this plant barely has a garlic smell and it doesn't taste strong, either. I have seen it in such profusion along southern roadsides that it almost forms a mat.

14 Cherry Laurel
Prunus caroliniana

This southern evergreen cherry has lovely white flowers and black fruit. You can find it in the woods from North Carolina on south. It is easily recognized by the shiny leaves and thickly clustered flowers.

15 Grape Hyacinth
Muscari botryoides

This early spring flowering bulb immigrated from southern Europe and Asia and was so happy in the South that it now grows wild in open fields and grassy areas. Its species name comes from the Greek meaning "a bunch of grapes," which is exactly what the flower cluster resembles.

16 Green and Gold
Chrysogonum virginianum

Early in the season this pretty little harbinger of spring seems almost stemless, for its flower pushes right past the leaves which seem to lie flat on the ground. But later on, the stem may grow as tall as two feet. Look for it in light rich woods and open places. It's so pretty that it is often cultivated and used for borders in gardens.

17 Southern Blue Flag
Iris virginica

This large blue iris can be found in open wet fields, ditches and swamps. It is a handsome plant that is particularly striking because the flower stands up above the leaves. The iris flower is used as a model for the fleur-de-lys chosen by King Louis VII for the royal coat of arms.

18 Cherokee Rose
Rosa laevigata

Long ago, the climbing Cherokee Rose was brought to America from China and was planted so widely all over the South that it is now often considered a native — and a most welcome and fragrant one at that. It is the state flower of Georgia.

19 Gaillardia, Fire Wheel
Gaillardia pulchella

This bright daisy-like flower was named after a French botanist, Gaillard de Marentonneau, and one variety came to the South as a garden flower. It liked its new habitat so well that it escaped to live on its own wherever it could find a nice sandy place — on beaches, dunes and roadsides. It has been used in herbal medicines as a facial balm. It is also called "Fire Wheel," which is what it looks like.

20 Southern Magnolia
Magnolia grandiflora

This magnificent plant with its distinctive perfume and spectacular flowers that grow as large as twelve inches across has long been associated with the South in story and song. And rightly so, for it is a native southern plant; although it is widely planted all over the U.S., it doesn't grow wild north of North Carolina. It is the state flower of Louisiana and Mississippi.

21 Yellow Jessamine
Gelsemium sempervirens

Like the Magnolia, the Yellow Jessamine is indigenous to the South. And like the Magnolia, it is impressively beautiful. The large yellow flowers bloom in profusion from semi-evergreen leaves, and send a marvelous fragrance into the air. It blossoms in the spring and transforms thickets and roadsides into gardens. A tea made from the flowers was thought to be good for coughs, pleurisy, stomach pains, and childbirth pains. It is the state flower of South Carolina.

22 Wisteria
Wisteria frutescens

Everyone can easily recognize wisteria because of its hanging bunches of purple flowers. They bloom in the spring and climb over trees and bushes throughout the South — from Virginia to Florida, and west to Arkansas.

23 Rosebay
Rhododendron maximum

If you have ever been to Savannah, Georgia, you will know how beautiful this flower is, blooming in all colors around the reconstructed squares there. It is also a breathtaking sight throughout the South in spring, when you see it in woods, or along streams. No wonder West Virginia chose it as the state flower. This large-leaved evergreen shrub grows on moist wooded bluffs and along stream banks in the mountains, mainly below 3,000 feet. The pink to white flowers with green spots on the largest petal are open in June.

24 Azalea
Rhododendron spp.

Visit most any southern city in March and you'll see just how beautiful these azaleas in all sizes and colors can be. But don't try to figure out the species of each. About eight or nine are native to the Southeast and they've mixed with one another. Others have been introduced from Asia and still others have been developed horticulturally. So just enjoy them and feel envious that this flower we must work so hard to cultivate further north grows here in wild profusion.

25 Pawpaw
Asimna triloba

Early spring brings forth the dull purple flower of the Pawpaw shrub before the leaves come out. Later on, the sweet smelling fruit develops. This fruit is said to be edible, although I have never tried it. The fruit juice and crushed seeds have been used to treat head lice.

26 Sassafras
Sassafras albidum

The Sassafras — which blooms in March before the leaves appear — is a very interesting and useful tree. Its roots were once used to make a tea thought to "bring out" the rash in measles. More recently — and more popularly — they are used to flavor rootbeer. Its young leaves are powdered and used to flavor the famous Louisiana gumbo soup. Extracts from the bark are used commercially to flavor toothpaste, soft drinks and many kinds of candy. The fruit is popular with squirrels and the powdered root is said to rid dogs and cats of fleas. In other words, it is a kitchen cupboard of a tree.

27 Wild Ginger, Heart Leaf
Hexastylis shuttleworthii

This is one of several kinds of wild ginger, worth looking for in the spring because of the unusual shape of the leaf. The roots are used in making a tea that is "good for you" although it does not have a very appealing taste. A cough medicine has been made by mixing the tea with lemon and whiskey. The particular wild ginger depicted is found in the Blue Ridge Mountains of North Carolina.

28 Periwinkle
Vinca minor

This lovely little flower has sad associations through history. In the Middle Ages in Europe, garlands were made of it to adorn the dead and the heads of people on their way to execution. It came to the South from England and was planted over graves, so you will now find it growing wild in old cemeteries. Often when gravestones have disappeared, "the periwinkle trails its wreaths" to mark old resting places with its evergreen leaves and delicate blue-purple flowers.

29 Trumpet Honeysuckle
Lonicera sempervirens

A southern vine of brilliant color, this honeysuckle creeps over walls and trees in late spring. There is a marked increase in the number of pink and red flowers as spring progresses, perfectly timed for the return of the hummingbird and the appearance of the butterflies; both are attracted by the bright colors. The honeysuckle has been associated since Shakespeare's time with love and maidens' bowers. It liked the South so well, it went wild here, but it is so attractive many people have put it back in their gardens.

30 Spiderwort
Tradescantia virginiana

Spiderwort got its common name because it was believed to cure spider bites. Its Latin name comes from John Tradescant, the famous gardener of Charles I. The flower is an immigrant from England that has gone wild in the South, although it is still a garden flower in the North. Old flower books compare Spiderwort to the dragonfly because its beauty is so short lived. It opens in the morning, withers in the afternoon and turns to a fluid jelly that gives the plant another common name — Widow's Tears.

31 Florida Violet
Viola floridana

It's fun to see how many different kinds of violets you can find. This particular one was first identified in Florida (which gave it its name) and spread throughout the South. Look for it during March and April, for its velvety purple flower pushes up in rich woods and wet places. The violet is almost as popular with poets as the rose — and seems all the more cherished for its tininess.

32 Low Bush Blackberry, Southern Dewberry
Rubus trivialis

This blackberry grows in waste sandy places from Virginia to Florida, and west to Texas. The fruit is black and sweet. The large flowers are quite profuse and draw attention to this trailing plant. But the prickles can cause you discomfort if you're not careful.

33 Jack-in-the-Pulpit
Arisaema triphyllum

This plant is also called Indian Turnip. The tube of the spathe (pulpit) is often deeply corrugated with green and purple stripes curving all the way to the tip of the hood. "Jack" is the spadix standing up in the spathe giving his muffled sermon: "Don't pick me." His message should be learned by all, for most spring wild flowers are becoming scarce even if they seem profuse in the area where you find them.

34 Great Solomon's Seal
Polygonatum canaliculatum

This large and very handsome plant grows over most of eastern North America. The flowers are greenish bells hanging below the leaves, but the leaves themselves are a handsome part of the plant. It is said that the nearly starved French colonists in North America were kept alive by eating the roots of this plant. If so, it must have been more plentiful three centuries ago than it is now.

35 False Solomon's Seal
Smilacina racemosa

The flowers of this plant grow at the end of the stalk and are a yellowish collection of little stars. Later, the berries develop and are an unusual brown-purple that changes to red as the season goes on. I painted both here just to show how they look.

36 Cardinal Flower
Lobelia cardinalis

When the brilliant red of the Cardinal Flower appears on the edges of lakes and streams, it is usually a sign that summer has nearly passed. It is a brave and beautiful farewell, because few sights are as lovely and rare as that of the Cardinal Flower standing in black water against the dark mysterious woods. Interestingly, it has been used to make medicine, but actually it should be considered poisonous, because it can cause death. The "lobelia" part of the Latin name comes from Mathe Lobel, a Flemish botanist who was the doctor of James I of England.

37 Indian Pipe
Monotropa uniflora

Indian Pipe grows all over North America, and you can find it in Japan and the Himalayas. It is quite a remarkable flower since it is leafless, and its stem is covered with scales — all that can be found of what might have once been leaves — and the plant doesn't even have any green color. The whole plant is whitish, and looks so ghostly that it has also been called Corpse Plant. Its popular name comes from its close resemblance to a small tobacco pipe when it is held horizontally. An extract of Indian Pipe was once recommended as a cure for eye irritations.

38 Viper's Bugloss
Echium vulgare

Farmers hate this plant as a pesky weed and have damned it with the name Bluedevils. But a distant field of them is a delight for anyone who treasures nature. Pink buds become bluish-purple and reddish-purple flowers. It was believed to cure snakebites because the seed resembles the head of a snake — the recipe called for eating the root while drinking wine. The Greek word "echium" means viper.

39 Twisted-Stalk
Streptopus amplexifolius

This pretty delicate spring flower blooms from May through July. The small bell-like flowers hang from under the leaves which in turn clasp around the stem. **Streptopus** in Greek actually means "twisted foot" although it is, as the English name suggests, actually the stalk that seems to change direction at each leaf joint. An unusual and lovely little flower.

40 Poison Ivy
Rhus radicans

Including Poison Ivy in a book about wild flowers may seem peripheral to botanists, but so many new explorers of the woods and fields cannot recognize it that a warning is important. Only someone who has suffered the misery of the itchy, blistery, spreading rash can imagine how uncomfortable the irritation can be — and you can get it by simply rubbing against any part of the plant. Recognize it by its shiny leaves that come in threes and look a little like ivy. It is a vine that spreads along the ground, climbs trees, and is, unfortunately, very common nearly everywhere.

41 Golden Alexander
Zizia aurea

Look for the lovely bright Golden Alexander along roadsides, in fields and swamps from April to June. The flowers dry well, incidentally, and have been used to make a strong, dull yellow dye. It is also known as the "golden meadow parsnip."

42 Dwarf Ginseng
Panax trifolium

This is a tiny version of the famous Ginseng plant which became almost extinct in North America because of exports; it is popular with Chinese all over the world as a cure for everything that may ail one. It has recently come into vogue in North America also and is now grown commercially here. **Panax** literally means a "cure for all ills." This pretty, small, rare plant may be found in rich woods in springtime.

43 Squirrel-Corn
Dicentra canadensis

The "corn" in the name comes from the shape of the yellow tubers in the root which look like grains of corn. There is some disagreement among botanists as to whether squirrels actually eat these or not. But none about the flower. It is lovely — nodding and fragrant — to examine close up, and just as lovely spread in a patch in the woods in springtime.

44 Blue-Eyed Grass
Sisyrinchium angustifolium

The Greek name for this delicate flower is "pig snout" because pigs dig up the roots. "Blue-Eyed Grass" is a better description, because it is a stiff upright grass with very tiny flowers that are actually the smallest in the iris family. The flower opens at sunrise and closes later in the day. Don't try to pick it, however, as the flower closes immediately — giving it natural protection.

45 Queen Anne's Lace
Daucus carota

Although it is a common weed that blooms in dry fields and along roadsides all summer long, it is so pretty that it is often added to flower arrangements when a dainty lacy look is wanted. It is also called "wild carrot" because that is precisely what the plant is; our common eating carrot was developed from it. You can still eat the root of wild carrot, but too much of it is said to turn the skin a jaundiced color.

46 Dandelion
Taraxacum officinale

One of our most wonderful wild plants —
pretty to look at and delicious to eat —
is one of the most maligned. People who
like their lawns to look like astroturf attack
it with chemicals and spades. Wiser
gardeners plant it — use the fresh leaves
in salad, cook them as valuable greens,
make wine from the flowers, roast the
roots to make a caffein-free coffee —
and at the same time have a very handsome
flower bed. And what is prettier to hold
and blow on than the exquisite ball of
feathery seeds? The English name comes
from **dent de lion** because the leaves were
thought to resemble a lion's teeth. But
the popular French name for the plant is
pissenlit, perhaps because children have
passed on the superstition that if you
pick a dandelion you'll wet the bed that
night.

47 Hobble Bush
Viburnum alnifolium

It is also called Moose Bush or Moose Wood, but I like still another name: American Wayfaring Tree. In the South it grows only in the highest mountain areas. The blossoms come early in spring. The large white flowers around the edges of the cluster are sterile — but are said to be useful in attracting insects to the small, insignificant-looking fertile flowers in the center.

48 Hawthorn
Crataegus flabellata

This handsome flowering shrub, more common in the North, is frequently found in the woods and fields of the South. There are many varieties of hawthorn, but even botanists have difficulty distinguishing them, so just be happy to recognize it by the zigzag twigs, the unbranched thorns and deciduous leaves. The blossoms are white and large, and the fruit like small apples. Although you can eat it, the stone is so large that you might as well leave it all for the birds, or use it for jelly. It is the state flower of Missouri.

THE WILD ORCHIDS

The rarest and most prized of all the wild flowers are the orchids, distinguished by their slipper-like petals. Not only does one never, never pick a wild orchid, but one does not tell where or when an orchid has been found in case somebody goes and picks it. Once in a while one comes across an unexpected mass of them, and then one feels privileged indeed.

49 White-fringed Orchis
Habenaria blephariglottis

Consider yourself very lucky if you come across this lovely orchid, as it is now very rare. The fringe around the lip makes it quite distinctive. It grows in sphagnum moss, near bogs, and in very wet fields, and blooms in July.

50 Pink Lady's Slipper
Cypripedium acaule

The Pink Lady's Slipper is one of the more common members of the orchid family. You may come upon great masses of it when walking in the open pine woods, and a lovely sight it is. Even though they seem plentiful, the flowers should not be picked, nor even transplanted, as they will seldom survive a change of habitat more than a few years.

51 White Lady's Slipper
Cypripedium acaule

The White Lady's Slipper is the same as the pink one, except that the slipper is pure white and remains so. Sometimes the Pink Lady's Slipper is pale pink one year and a darker deeper pink another, but if you stake the white one and revisit it another year, it will still be white. It is also much rarer than the pink.

52 Showy Orchis
Orchis spectabilis

This little four to twelve-inch orchid is also quite rare, and very pretty. The purple hood contrasts with the white lip when it blooms in May in rich woods, usually in quite wet places beloved by mosquitoes. Nineteenth century books on flowers also claim it to be quite rare. Although more common in the North, you may be lucky to find it along streams in the Piedmont and mountains.

Index — English

Anemone, Rue 10
Azalea 24
Blackberry, Low Bush 32
Blue-Eyed Grass 44
Blue Flag, Southern 17
Cardinal Flower 36
Cinquefoil, Dwarf 12
Dandelion 46
Dewberry, Southern 32
Dogwood, Flowering 6
Fire Wheel 19
Gaillardia 19
Garlic, False 13
Ginger, Wild 27
Ginseng, Dwarf 42
Golden Alexander 41
Green and Gold 16
Hawthorn 48
Heart Leaf 27
Hobble Bush 47
Honeysuckle, Trumpet 29
Hyacinth, Grape 15
Hyacinth, Wild 9
Indian Pipe 37
Iris, Crested Dwarf 5
Jack-in-the-Pulpit 33
Jessamine, Yellow 21
Lady's Slipper, Pink 50, White 51
Laurel, Cherry 14
Magnolia, Southern 20
Orchis, Showy 52
Orchis, White-fringed 49
Pawpaw 25
Pennywort, Marsh 8
Periwinkle 28
Poison Ivy 40
Prickly Pear 4
Queen Anne's Lace 45
Rose, Cherokee 18
Rosebay 23
Sassafras 26
Solomon's Seal, Great 34
Solomon's Seal, False 35
Sorrel 3
Sorrel, Pink, Violet Wood 1
Spiderwort 30
Spring-Beauty 11
Squirrel-Corn 43
Star Flower, Spring 2
Toadflax 7
Twisted-Stalk 39
Violet, Florida 31
Viper's Bugloss 38
Wisteria 22

Index — Latin

Anemonella thalictroides 10
Arisaema triphyllum 33
Asimna triloba 25
Camassia scilloides 9
Chrysogonum virginianum 16
Claytonia virginica 11
Cornus florida 6
Crataegus flabellata 48
Cypripedium acaule 50, 51
Daucus carota 45
Dicentra canadensis 43
Echium vulgare 38
Gaillardia pulchella 19
Gelsemium sempervirens 21
Habenaria blephariglottis 49
Hexastylis shuttleworthii 27
Hydrocotyle umbellata 8
Ipheion uniflorum 2
Iris cristata 5
Iris virginica 17
Linaria canadensis 7
Lobelia cardinalis 36
Lonicera sempervirens 29
Magnolia grandiflora 20
Monotropa uniflora 37
Muscari botryoides 15
Nothoscordum bivalve 13
Opuntia compressa 4
Orchis spectabilis 52
Oxalis violacea 1
Panax trifolium 42
Polygonatum canaliculatum 34
Potentilla canadensis 12
Prunus caroliniana 14
Rhododendron maximum 23
Rhododendron spp. 24
Rhus radicans 40
Rosa laevigata 18
Rubus trivialis 32
Rumex hastatulus 3
Sassafras albidum 26
Sisyrinchium angustifolium 44
Smilacina racemosa 35
Streptopus amplexifolius 39
Taraxacum officinale 46
Tradescantia virginiana 30
Viburnum alnifolium 47
Vinca minor 28
Viola floridana 31
Wisteria frutescens 22
Zizia aurea 41

Photo: Mary Landry

Katherine Mackenzie was introduced to wild flowers by her father during summers on the Lower St. Lawrence. When she started to paint the flowers she had the tutelage of Patrick Morgan, the New York artist and naturalist, who created one of Quebec's most beautiful gardens at Murray Bay and was responsible for the new plantings and pool at the New York Botanical Gardens. She has traveled throughout eastern North America to paint wild flowers as far north as Devon Island in the High Arctic, and she is presently on a painting tour in Mexico.

Her house is an old farm house in Eastern Quebec, on the Vermont border, where she has been involved in creating a wild flower preserve. She is a member of several American, British and Canadian horticultural societies as well as the Arctic Institute of North America and the Smithsonian Institute.